D1518280

INSIDE THE NHL

Vancouver Canucks

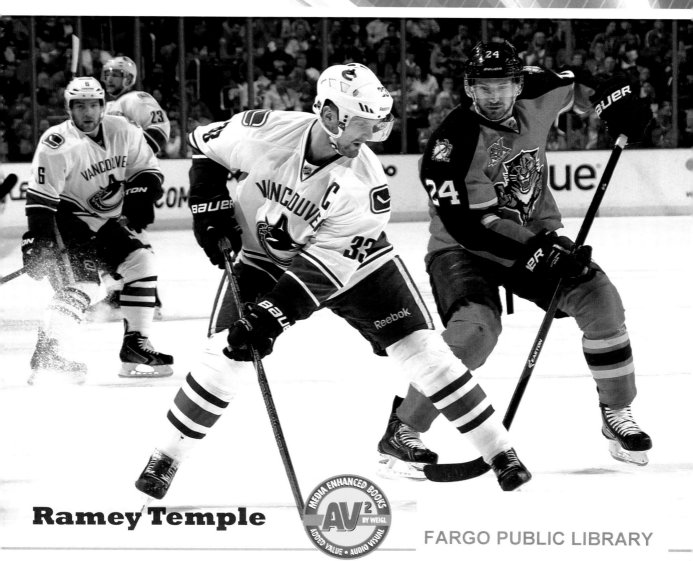

Ramey Temple

AV2 MEDIA ENHANCED BOOKS
BY WEIGL
ADDED VALUE • AUDIO VISUAL

www.av2books.com

AV² provides enriched content that supplements and complements this book. Weigl's AV² books strive to create inspired learning and engage young minds in a total learning experience.

Your AV² Media Enhanced books come alive with...

Audio
Listen to sections of the book read aloud.

Key Words
Study vocabulary, and complete a matching word activity.

Video
Watch informative video clips.

Quizzes
Test your knowledge.

Embedded Weblinks
Gain additional information for research.

Slide Show
View images and captions, and prepare a presentation.

Try This!
Complete activities and hands-on experiments.

... and much, much more!

Go to **www.av2books.com**, and enter this book's unique code.

BOOK CODE

R 7 6 9 3 2 5

AV² by Weigl brings you media enhanced books that support active learning.

Published by AV² by Weigl
350 5th Avenue, 59th Floor
New York, NY 10118
Websites: www.av2books.com   www.weigl.com

Library of Congress Control Number: 2014951939

ISBN 978-1-4896-3191-6 (hardcover)
ISBN 978-1-4896-4019-2 (softcover)
ISBN 978-1-4896-3192-3 (single-user eBook)
ISBN 978-1-4896-3193-0 (multi-user eBook)

Printed in the United States of America in Brainerd, Minnesota
1 2 3 4 5 6 7 8 9 0 19 18 17 16 15

032015
WEP050315

Senior Editor Heather Kissock
Art Director Terry Paulhus

Photo Credits
Every reasonable effort has been made to trace ownership and to obtain permission to reprint copyright material. The publishers would be pleased to have any errors or omissions brought to their attention so that they may be corrected in subsequent printings.

Weigl acknowledges Getty Images and iStock as its primary image suppliers for this title.

Vancouver Canucks

CONTENTS

Introduction

The Vancouver Canucks were originally part of the **Pacific Coast Hockey League (PCHL)**, in which they began play in 1945. The Canucks nickname was taken from Canadian folk hero Johnny Canuck, who was a great logger and a part-time hockey player. Joining the NHL's East Division in 1970, the Canucks finished dead last, as most **expansion** teams do. By 1974, the Canucks joined the Smythe Division and were the surprise of the league, finishing in first place and winning the division.

Henrik Sedin holds the team record for career points.

Their first **playoff series** pitted them against the Montreal Canadiens, who beat them easily, four games to one. During the next 39 seasons, the Canucks found themselves in the postseason 25 times, and in the Stanley Cup Final three times. They have yet to capture the Cup, but the Canucks have been on quite a roll recently, winning their division in each season from 2009 to 2013.

Alex Burrows is known as an aggressive player, having served close to 1,000 career penalty minutes.

Vancouver
CANUCKS

Arena Rogers Arena

Division Pacific

Head Coach Willie Desjardins

Location Vancouver, British Columbia, Canada

NHL Stanley Cup Titles None

Nicknames The Nucks, The Canuckleheads

3 Conference Finals

2 Presidents' Trophies

10 Division Championships

26 Playoff Appearances

History

Stan Smyl's jersey was retired by the Canucks on November 3, 1991.

The roots of hockey in Vancouver began more than a century ago with the Vancouver Millionaires, a team that competed in the Pacific Coast Hockey Association and Western Canada Hockey League between 1911 and 1926. The Canucks arrived in 1945 as a minor league hockey team with a big fan following. After failing to become one of the first expansion teams in 1967, the Canucks entered the NHL during the second round of expansion in 1970.

Under interim coach Roger Neilson, the Canucks made an unlikely playoff run in 1982, and found themselves staring across the ice at the two-time defending champions, the New York Islanders, with a chance to win the Stanley Cup. The Canucks came up empty though, losing all four games.

They made it back again in 1994 against the New York Rangers and were defeated in the seventh and deciding game. In 2011, the Canucks were back in the final for a third time, when they would come up short against a feisty Bruins team. The next time the Canucks reach the final, they plan to take home the Cup.

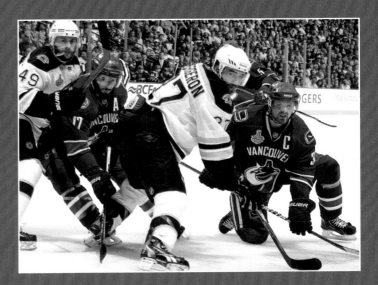

The Canucks won three out of seven games in the 2011 Stanley Cup Final.

The Arena

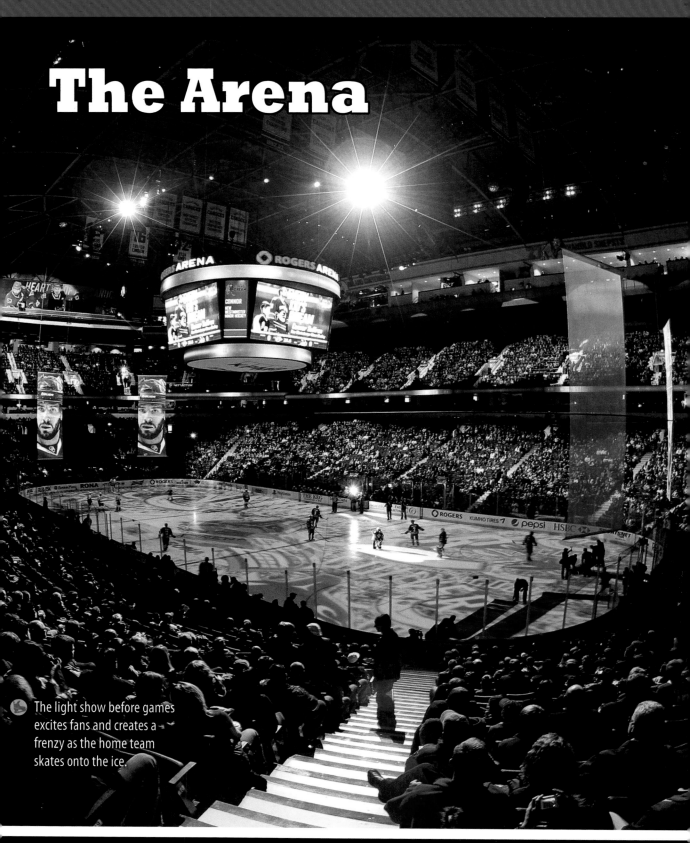

The light show before games excites fans and creates a frenzy as the home team skates onto the ice.

The Rogers Arena first opened on September 21, 1995, funded by General Motors of Canada. The arena holds about 19,056 during Canucks games. Rogers Arena is the former home of the Vancouver Grizzlies, a National Basketball Association (NBA) **franchise** that moved to Memphis in 2001, and the Vancouver Ravens of the National Lacrosse League (NLL). The arena has many uses. It can be changed from an ice rink to a concert venue, and even to an indoor tennis court.

Rogers Arena replaced the Pacific Coliseum, which was the first building the Canucks played in, beginning in 1970. Before the Canucks signed a **sponsorship** deal with Rogers Communications in 2010, the facility was called General Motors Place, but was nicknamed "The Garage" because General Motors is a large automobile company. The arena has a great location, right in the heart of downtown Vancouver.

In 2001, the arena hosted the World Figure Skating Championships. However, the highlight for Rogers Arena took place in 2011, when it played host to the Stanley Cup Final.

Rogers Arena hosts many concerts, including a 2014 performance by singer Demi Lovato.

Where They Play

British Columbia

Alberta

CANADA

4

Manitoba

Ontario

Saskatchewan

3

14

Rogers Arena, Vancouver

7

Washington

Montana

North Dakota

Minnesota

11

Wisconsin

Oregon

Idaho

South Dakota

8

Iowa

UNITED

Wyoming

Nebraska

Illinois

6

Nevada

Utah

Colorado

9

Kansas

Missouri

13

California

STATES

5

Oklahoma

Arkansas

1

Arizona

2

New Mexico

Texas

10

Mississi[ppi]

Pacific Ocean

MEXICO

Louisiana

Gulf of Mexico

NHL WESTERN CONFERENCE

PACIFIC DIVISION

1	Anaheim Ducks	5	Los Angeles Kings
2	Arizona Coyotes	6	San Jose Sharks
3	Calgary Flames	★ 7	Vancouver Canucks
4	Edmonton Oilers		

CENTRAL DIVISION

8	Chicago Blackhawks	12	Nashville Predators
9	Colorado Avalanche	13	St. Louis Blues
10	Dallas Stars	14	Winnipeg Jets
11	Minnesota Wild		

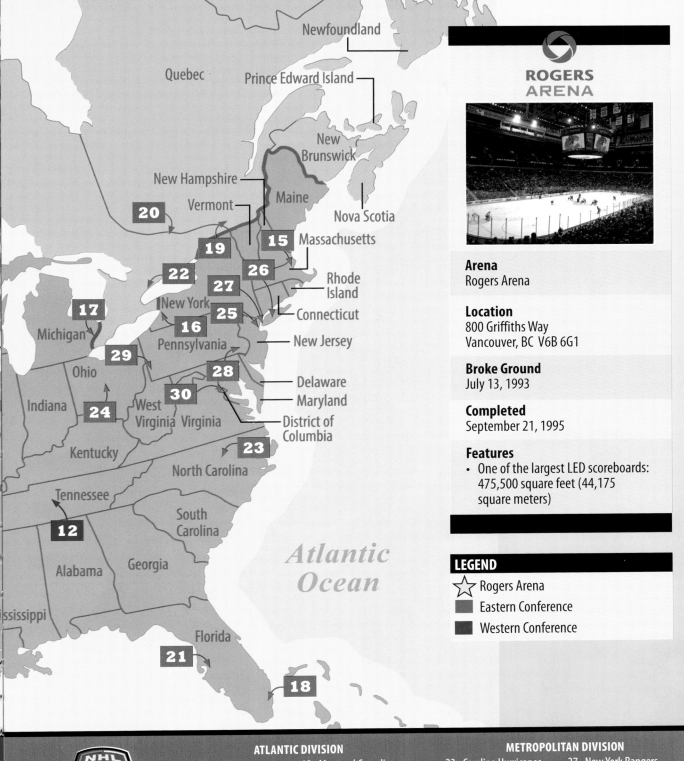

Newfoundland

Quebec

Prince Edward Island

New Brunswick

New Hampshire

20

Vermont

Maine

19

15 Massachusetts

22

26

Nova Scotia

27

Rhode Island

17

New York

25

Connecticut

Michigan

16

New Jersey

Pennsylvania

Ohio

29

Indiana

24

30

Delaware

West Virginia Virginia

28

Maryland

District of Columbia

Kentucky

23

North Carolina

Tennessee

South Carolina

12

Alabama Georgia

Mississippi

Atlantic Ocean

Florida

21

18

ROGERS ARENA

Arena
Rogers Arena

Location
800 Griffiths Way
Vancouver, BC V6B 6G1

Broke Ground
July 13, 1993

Completed
September 21, 1995

Features
- One of the largest LED scoreboards: 475,500 square feet (44,175 square meters)

LEGEND
☆ Rogers Arena
▮ Eastern Conference
▮ Western Conference

ATLANTIC DIVISION

15 Boston Bruins
16 Buffalo Sabres
17 Detroit Red Wings
18 Florida Panthers
19 Montreal Canadiens
20 Ottawa Senators
21 Tampa Bay Lightning
22 Toronto Maple Leafs

METROPOLITAN DIVISION

23 Carolina Hurricanes
24 Columbus Blue Jackets
25 New Jersey Devils
26 New York Islanders
27 New York Rangers
28 Philadelphia Flyers
29 Pittsburgh Penguins
30 Washington Capitals

The Uniforms

V The Vancouver Millionaires had a famous "V" shaped symbol on the front of their jersey, something that was used again in 1982 when the Canucks changed uniforms.

The 2007 Canucks uniform features one new color. Silver was added to the trim around the logo.

The Canucks have changed their uniforms many times since 1970. They originally wore blue, green, and white uniforms, but switched to orange, black, and red uniforms in 1978. To this day, the 1978 uniforms are still recognized as one of the wildest uniforms in NHL history.

HOME

As of 2007, the Canucks' uniforms returned to their roots of blue, green, and white. They used the old "stick in rink" **logo** for the alternate jersey and the new Canuck "C-shaped" logo for the standard jerseys. The team has jerseys of two different colors for home and away games, a blue jersey and a white jersey. The uniform pants are also either blue or white.

AWAY

During the 2006 season, Richard Park and the Canucks wore their "stick in rink" jerseys.

Helmets and Face Masks

Goalies are allowed to decorate their helmets with **SPECIAL DESIGNS** that may or may not relate to the team.

Goalies must wear extra padding on their body and extra protection on their faces in order to guard against injury.

The Vancouver Canucks' helmets are blue and white to match their uniforms. The helmets have no patterns on them. As of 1979, helmets are required for position players to help prevent injuries. The team's helmets come in two different colors, blue for home games and white for away.

Goalies are allowed to wear special helmets that have unique designs. The special design of goalie helmets has become a favorite discussion topic among fans. Canucks goalie Eddie Lack decorated his goalie mask with mountains, as well as the original Canucks logo, on the left side. The helmet is mostly blue and green and resembles the Canadian wilderness. This helmet was designed by a 14-year-old boy who submitted the winning design to a contest the Canucks sponsored. Another Canucks goalie, Corey Hirsch, decorated his mask with images from the horror film *Psycho*.

Experienced players, like Daniel Sedin, have the option of wearing a protective visor on their helmet. For new players entering the league, wearing the visor is mandatory.

The Coaches

0 Years of NHL coaching experience for new head coach Willie Desjardins

Willie Desjardins will try to lead the Canucks to a new playoff streak. The team's last playoff streak was 2009 to 2013.

The Canucks have had 20 different coaches throughout their 44-year history. Each of these coaches has contributed to the team in some way. The Canucks have come a long way from the expansion club that head coach Hal Laycoe brought to the ice in 1970. Appearing in three Stanley Cup Finals, yet never bringing home the Cup, has made the Canucks hungry for their first championship.

ALAIN VIGNEAULT Alain Vigneault coached the Canucks for seven seasons, earning more wins than any coach in franchise history. Vigneault won the Jack Adams Award as the top coach of the year in 2006–2007. Vigneault and the Canucks captured back-to-back Presidents' Trophies in 2011 and 2012, as the team with the best regular season record in the NHL. Vigneault also led the Canucks to the Stanley Cup Final in 2011, where they lost to the Bruins.

PAT QUINN Pat Quinn, "The Big Irishman," served as both the general manager and head coach for the Canucks. In 1994, he coached the seventh-**seeded** Canucks to an unlikely run to the Stanley Cup Final, where they lost in seven games to the New York Rangers.

WILLIE DESJARDINS Willie Desjardins became the 20th head coach of the Canucks in 2014. Desjardins is a unique coach, who encourages players to voice their opinions and provide feedback on everything from game strategy to **line** decisions. The immediate task for Desjardins is to improve the Canucks' **power play**, as they were 26th in the NHL with a one-man advantage during the 2013–2014 season.

Fans and the Internet

Fans often dress up and paint their faces blue and green to show support for the Canucks.

NHL teams are well known for having energetic and passionate fans. Among the most famous NHL fan traditions is one that began in 1982 when the Canucks hosted the Chicago Blackhawks in Vancouver. Fans began waving white towels in the air—some of which were tied to hockey sticks. The towel waving caught on and can now be seen at home games throughout the league, and beyond, in various other sports.

Fans visiting the Canucks' official website will find articles, photos, social media connections, and a team store. For an even more in-depth view of the team, many fans follow two of the top Canucks blogs, which are Canucks Army and Nucks Misconduct. Both websites offer a community for fans to talk, and occasionally argue, about anything and everything related to the Canucks.

Signs
of a fan

#1 True Canucks fans can download Canucks Mobile, the official team app, which offers in-game scoring alerts, statistics, and player profiles.

#2 The Canucks website offers a Letter to the Editor section, where fans can write in and share their point of view.

Legends of the Past

Many great players have suited up for the Canucks. A few of them have become icons of the team and the city it represents.

Pavel Bure

Pavel Bure was given the nickname "The Russian Rocket" because of his incredible speed on the ice. He was chosen in the sixth round of the 1989 NHL **Entry Draft** amid controversy, as he was supposedly not eligible to play in the NHL for another season. During his first season with the Canucks, in 1991, Bure scored 60 points in just 65 games, and won the Calder Memorial Trophy as **Rookie** of the Year. He scored 254 goals in seven seasons with the Canucks, and led them to the Stanley Cup Final in 1994. His dominance became legend in that postseason, as he scored 16 goals and had seven **assists** during 24 playoff games.

Position: Right Wing
NHL Seasons: 12 (1991–2003)
Born: March 31, 1971, in Moscow, Soviet Union

Trevor Linden

Trevor Linden played for the Canucks for 16 seasons. He is the all-time Canucks leader in games played, and is among the top five in virtually every team offensive category. In 1994, the talented center and right wing led the Canucks to the Stanley Cup Final. He won the King Clancy Memorial Trophy in 1997 as a humanitarian and a leader, and was named to the Maclean's Honor Roll in 2004 as a Canadian who made a difference. He is currently the president of the Canucks. The Canucks retired Linden's jersey, number 16, in 2008.

Position: Center/Right Wing
NHL Seasons: 19 (1988–2008)
Born: April 11, 1970, in Medicine Hat, Alberta, Canada

Markus Naslund

Markus Naslund is a highly skilled offensive player known for his speed and puck handling. In 2000, he became the first European-born team captain in Canucks history. The four-time **All-Star** was drafted by the Penguins in 1991, but was traded just a few years later to the Canucks in what would go down as one of the most lopsided trades in NHL history. Naslund ended up playing 12 of his 16 NHL seasons for the Canucks, scoring 756 points. The Penguins received Alek Stojanov in return for Naslund. Stojanov scored just six points in a disappointing two-season NHL career.

Position: Left Wing
NHL Seasons: 15 (1993–2009)
Born: July 30, 1973, in Ornskoldsvik, Sweden

Stan Smyl

Stan Smyl spent his entire 13-year career with the Canucks. He is currently a scout and senior advisor to the general manager in Vancouver. On the day he retired in 1991, Smyl was the team leader in games played at 896, assists at 411, and points at 673. That same day, he was hired as the Canucks' assistant coach. Smyl is often described as the heart and soul of the Canucks because of his enthusiasm and leadership. He was the longest-serving team captain of the Canucks, and his jersey was retired in 1991.

Position: Right Wing
NHL Seasons: 13 (1978–1991)
Born: January 28, 1958, in Glendon, Alberta, Canada

Stars of Today

oday's Canucks team is made up of many young, talented players who have proven that they are among the best in the league.

Henrik Sedin

enrik Sedin was the third overall pick in the 1999 NHL Entry Draft. He has played each of his 14 seasons with the Canucks and is in the process of rewriting the team record books. Sedin is best known for his passing, recording seven of the top 10 assist seasons in Canucks' history. He also holds the all-time Canucks assist record, with 650. In 2006, Sedin played for the Swedish Olympic team in Torino, where he helped bring home a gold medal against Finland. His identical twin brother, Daniel Sedin, also plays for the Canucks as a winger.

Position: Center
NHL Seasons: 14 (2000–Present)
Born: September 26, 1980, in Ornskoldsvik, Sweden

Daniel Sedin

aniel Sedin was drafted ahead of his twin brother, Henrik, as the second overall pick in the 1999 draft. Like his brother, Daniel has played all of his 14 NHL seasons with the Canucks. While Henrik is likely the better playmaker, Daniel is a more accomplished scorer. The seven-time All-Star scored a career best 41 goals in 2011, the same year the Canucks made a run to the Stanley Cup Final. Also in 2011, Sedin won the Art Ross Trophy as the highest point-scorer, with 104 points, as well as the Ted Lindsay Award, given to the best player in the league, as voted on by fellow players.

Position: Left Wing
NHL Seasons: 14 (2000–Present)
Born: September 26, 1980, in Ornskoldsvik, Sweden

Ryan Miller

Ryan Miller is an American goaltender who grew up in Michigan and went on to play hockey at Michigan State for four years. Miller is from a true hockey family, as his brother Drew and cousins Kelly, Kip, and Kevin all play in the NHL. All five Millers were Spartans, playing college hockey at Michigan State. Miller played 11 seasons with the Buffalo Sabres and one with the St. Louis Blues. The 2014–2015 season will mark his first as a Canuck. Miller had a career 2.59 **goals against average** before beginning his first season as a Canuck in 2014–2015.

Position: Goaltender
NHL Seasons: 12 (2002–Present)
Born: July 17, 1980, in East Lansing, Michigan, USA

Kevin Bieksa

Kevin Bieksa is an alternate captain and an aggressive defenseman for the Canucks. The Canadian is a four-time All-Star who has played all of his 10 NHL seasons in Vancouver. Bieksa was drafted by the Canucks in 2001 and played with the team's minor league **affiliate**, the Manitoba Moose, before joining the Canucks in 2005. His teammates call him "Juice" because he drinks so much of the stuff, and he is known throughout the league as one of the premier offensive-minded defensemen.

Position: Defenseman
NHL Seasons: 10 (2004–Present)
Born: June 16, 1981, in Grimsby, Ontario, Canada

All-Time Records

1,140
Most Games Played
Trevor Linden leads the Canucks in most games played, with 1,140. He is followed by both Sedin twins, Henrik and Daniel.

10
Most Hat Tricks
Markus Naslund recorded a team record 10 **hat tricks** as a Canuck. Pavel Bure, the Russian Rocket, finished his Vancouver days just behind Naslund, with nine hat tricks.

24
Short-handed Goals
Pavel Bure had 24 short-handed goals in just seven seasons with the Canucks.

346
Most Goals
Markus Naslund holds the record for most all-time goals, at 346, although Henrik Sedin is closing in on that record.

20.3
Best shooting percentage
Mike Walton has the best **shooting percentage** of all Canuck players, at 20.3 percent, meaning one in five of his career shots was a goal. He is followed by Darcy Rota and Petr Nedved.

Timeline

Throughout the team's history, the Canucks have had many memorable events that have become defining moments for the team and its fans.

1974
The Canucks are moved into the Smythe Division, where they are immediately more successful, making it to the playoffs for the first time. They are defeated in five games by the Canadiens.

1991
Pavel Bure, the Russian Rocket, finally joins the Canucks, after he is released from his contract with the Soviet Ice Hockey Federation. The rookie is sensational, leading the Canucks to the playoffs and winning the Calder Memorial Trophy as the Rookie of the Year.

| 1970 | 1974 | 1978 | 1982 | 1986 | 1990 |

1978
The Canucks undergo a uniform change when they ditch their old blue and green uniforms in favor of red, black, brown, and orange ones. These uniforms would become known as the boldest uniforms in NHL history.

1982
The Canucks make it to the Stanley Cup Final for the first time in team history. They are defeated by the Islanders.

In 1987, Pat Quinn is hired as the new president and general manager of the Canucks.

1997

The modern Canucks jersey is designed with the killer whale logo on front. This logo shows a whale breaking through the ice, a design that forms a "C" shape, representing the word "Canuck."

The Future

The Canucks' past is marked by great players and missed opportunities. They have made 26 playoff appearances and made it to the Stanley Cup Final three times, but have no championship to show for it. The Canucks have won their division every year from 2009 to 2013. Anchored by a core of young players and a deep tradition of winning, the Canucks are fighting to make certain that the next time they have an opportunity to win the Stanley Cup, they take it.

Roberto Luongo becomes the first Canuck goalie to be named captain since the PCHL Canucks had a goalie as their captain in 1947.

1998   **2002**   **2006**   **2010**   **2014**   **2018**

2010

Henrik Sedin becomes the first Canuck to win the Art Ross Trophy, scoring 112 points. Sedin is also named the new team captain.

2012

The Canucks win the Presidents' Trophy for the second season in a row, after having the best record in the NHL. They also capture first place in the Northwest Division for the fourth year in a row.

1994

The Canucks make it to the Stanley Cup Final once more. This time they are defeated by the New York Rangers.

Write a Biography

Life Story

A person's life story can be the subject of a book. This kind of book is called a biography. Biographies often describe the lives of people who have achieved great success. These people may be alive today, or they may have lived many years ago. Reading a biography can help you learn more about a great person.

Get the Facts

Use this book, and research in the library and on the internet, to find out more about your favorite Canuck. Learn as much about this player as you can. What position does he play? What are his statistics in important categories? Has he set any records? Also, be sure to write down key events in the person's life. What was his childhood like? What has he accomplished off the field? Is there anything else that makes this person special or unusual?

Use the Concept Web

A concept web is a useful research tool. Read the questions in the concept web on the following page. Answer the questions in your notebook. Your answers will help you write a biography.

Concept Web

Adulthood
- Where does this individual currently reside?
- Does he or she have a family?

Your Opinion
- What did you learn from the books you read in your research?
- Would you suggest these books to others?
- Was anything missing from these books?

Childhood
- Where and when was this person born?
- Describe his or her parents, siblings, and friends.
- Did this person grow up in unusual circumstances?

Accomplishments off the Field
- What is this person's life's work?
- Has he or she received awards or recognition for accomplishments?
- How have this person's accomplishments served others?

Write a Biography

Help and Obstacles
- Did this individual have a positive attitude?
- Did he or she receive help from others?
- Did this person have a mentor?
- Did this person face any hardships?
- If so, how were the hardships overcome?

Accomplishments on the Field
- What records does this person hold?
- What key games and plays have defined his career?
- What are his stats in categories important to his position?

Work and Preparation
- What was this person's education?
- What was his or her work experience?
- How does this person work?
- What is the process he or she uses?

Trivia Time

Take this quiz to test your knowledge of the Canucks. The answers are printed upside down under each question.

1 Who is the Canadian folk hero the Canucks are named after?

A. Johnny Canuck

2 Which player is known as the Russian Rocket?

A. Pavel Bure

3 Who was the 20th head coach of the Canucks?

A. Willie Desjardins

4 Which Canuck goalie played hockey at Michigan State?

A. Ryan Miller

5 How many playoff appearances have the Canucks made?

A. 26

6 What is the current name of the Canucks' arena?

A. Rogers Arena

7 Which team did the Canucks lose to in the 1982 Stanley Cup Final?

A. The New York Islanders

8 How many seasons did Stan Smyl play for the Canucks?

A. 13

9 In what year did the Canucks join the NHL?

A. 1970

Key Words

affiliate: a minor league team that works in connection with its parent hockey club, providing opportunities for players to develop and prepare for hockey on the NHL level

All-Star: a game made for the best-ranked players in the NHL that happens mid-season. A player can be named an All-Star and then be sent to play in this game.

assists: a statistic that is attributed to up to two players of the scoring team who shoot, pass, or deflect the puck toward the scoring teammate

entry draft: an annual meeting where different teams in the NHL are allowed to pick new, young players who can join their teams

expansion: expansion in the NHL is marked by the addition of a new franchise. The league last expanded in 2000 when the Columbus Blue Jackets and Minnesota Wild joined the NHL.

franchise: a team that is a member of a professional sports league

goals against average: a statistic that is the average of goals allowed per game by a goaltender

hat tricks: when a player scores three goals in one game

line: forwards who play in a group, or "shift," during a game

logo: a symbol that stands for a team or organization

Pacific Coast Hockey League (PCHL): an ice hockey minor league that existed in the western USA and western Canada

playoff series: a series of games that occur after regular season play

power play: when a player from one team is in the penalty box, the other team gains an advantage in the number of players

rookie: a player age 26 or younger who has played no more than 25 games in a previous season, nor six or more games in two previous seasons

seeded: a method of ranking teams for postseason play based on regular season records

shooting percentage: the rate at which a player's shots hitting the net actually go in

sponsorship: to support an NHL team financially in exchange for the promotion of a certain company's products or services

Index

Log on to www.av2books.com

AV² by Weigl brings you media enhanced books that support active learning. Go to www.av2books.com, and enter the special code found on page 2 of this book. You will gain access to enriched and enhanced content that supplements and complements this book. Content includes video, audio, weblinks, quizzes, a slide show, and activities.

AV² Online Navigation

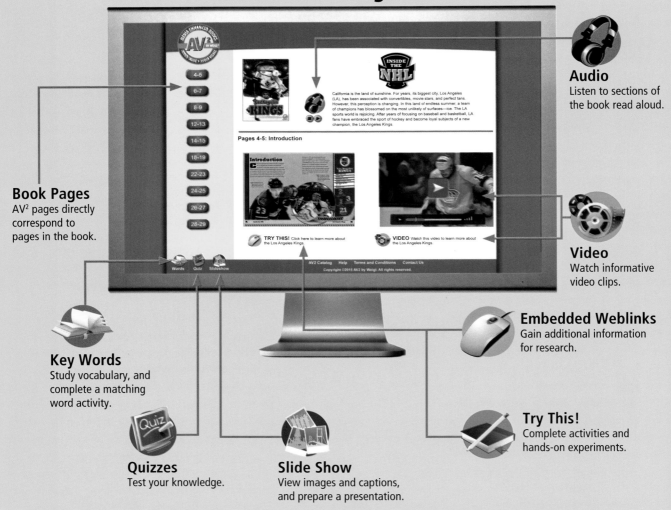

Book Pages
AV² pages directly correspond to pages in the book.

Audio
Listen to sections of the book read aloud.

Video
Watch informative video clips.

Embedded Weblinks
Gain additional information for research.

Key Words
Study vocabulary, and complete a matching word activity.

Try This!
Complete activities and hands-on experiments.

Quizzes
Test your knowledge.

Slide Show
View images and captions, and prepare a presentation.

AV² was built to bridge the gap between print and digital. We encourage you to tell us what you like and what you want to see in the future.

Sign up to be an AV² Ambassador at www.av2books.com/ambassador.